Pippa and Pop

Special Edition

Caroline Nixon & Michael Tomlinson

with Lesley Koustaff & Susan Rivers

CAMBRIDGE
UNIVERSITY PRESS

Map of the book

	VOCABULARY	LANGUAGE	SOUNDS AND LETTERS	LITERACY AND VALUES	NUMBERS	CROSS-CURRICULAR	PROJECT
Introduction Page 4							
1 **Me!** Page 6	Review Level 2: characters, numbers , likes *angry, bored, excited, scared, sleepy, surprised*	*Hello! What's your name? I'm (Kim). How old are you? I'm (eight). I like (books). What's her / his name? She's (Kim). He's (Dan). How old is she / he? She's / He's (eight).* *He's / She's / I'm (bored). He isn't / She isn't / I'm not (bored).*	Review Level 2 letter sounds: *b, m, t, g, p, d, k, n, s, h*	*Jane's name* Be yourself	Review numbers: *1–20*	Social studies: Identifying emotions from tone of voice	Make a self portrait
2 **My day** Page 18	*brush my hair, brush my teeth, get dressed, have breakfast, wake up, wash my face* *go to bed, have a bath, have dinner, have a snack, listen to a story, play with friends*	*I (wake up) (in the morning / every day).* *They / We (play with friends) (after school / in the evening). We / They don't (have a bath).*	Letter sound /ʃ / (sh)	*Brush your hair, Leo!* Look after yourself	Adding up by counting	Social studies: Times of day	Make a daily activities display
3 **My home** Page 30	*make the bed, pick up the toys, set the table, sweep the floor, wash the clothes, wash the dishes* *bed, bookcase, cupboard, lamp, rug, toy box*	*He / She (washes the dishes). I (sweep the floor).* *It's (under / in / on / next to) the (bed).*	Letter sound /k / (ck)	*Goldilocks and the three bears* Respect other people's things	Numbers: *10, 20, 30, 40*	Social studies: Objects at home	Make and decorate a bedroom
Units 1–3 Review Page 42–43							
4 **My sports** Page 44	*badminton, baseball, basketball, football, hockey, tennis* *bouncing, catching, hitting, kicking, rolling, throwing*	*They're / She's / He's playing (football) .* *She's / He's / They're / I'm (throwing) the ball.*	Letter sound /ŋ / (ng)	*A sport for Grace* Persevere	Subtracting by counting	Physical education: Team sports	Make a ball

	VOCABULARY	LANGUAGE	SOUNDS AND LETTERS	LITERACY AND VALUES	NUMBERS	CROSS-CURRICULAR	PROJECT
5 My free time Page 56	cooking dinner, drawing pictures, listening to singing, playing video games, reading books, watching TV go roller skating, go swimming, play a board game, play with building blocks, play hide-and-seek, play outside	I / We like (reading books). Let's (go swimming / play a board game)! Can I (come / play)?	Letter sounds / ʊ / (short oo) and / uː / (long oo)	Jack loves reading Join in and help	Numbers: 50, 60	Art: Paintings, photographs and sculptures	Make a board game
6 My food Page 68	cake, chocolate, crisps, grapes, pineapple, sweets beans, cereal, fruit, meat, rice, vegetables	Would you like some (chocolate)? Yes, please. / No, thank you. I'd like some (sweets), please. I / We have (meat and rice) for (breakfast / lunch / dinner).	Letter sound / tʃ / (ch)	Share, Ricky Raccoon! Share	Estimating quantity	Science: Salty, sour and sweet	Make a plate of food
Units 4–6 Review Page 80–81							
7 Animals Page 82	crocodile, elephant, hippo, monkey, snake, tiger duck, giraffe, lizard, parrot, spider, zebra	There's (a monkey). There are (three) (monkeys). There are (lots of) (snakes). They're (giraffes). They've got (long necks / long legs / stripes / short legs / big feet / long tails / sharp teeth). They're (fast).	Letter sound / θ / (th)	The bird and the lion Be friendly	Numbers: 70, 80	Science: Where animals live	Make an animal
8 Plants Page 94	garden, plants, rain, seeds, soil, sun beautiful, clean, dirty, new, old, ugly	What do plants need? Plants need (sun / rain / soil). What (beautiful) (flowers)! What (a dirty) (nose)!	Letter sound / iː / (ee, ea)	Sophia and Sam's garden Work together	Measuring length	Science: How plants grow	Make a plant diagram
9 My town Page 106	hospital, playground, restaurant, school, shop, supermarket doctor, farmer, nurse, shop assistant, teacher, waiter	Where are you / are we going? I'm / We're going to the (supermarket). A (teacher) works in a (school). He / She works on a farm. Where does (a teacher) work? Does (a nurse) work (in) a (hospital)? Yes, he / she does. No, he / she doesn't.	Letter sound / eɪ / (ay, ai)	Big-city cat and small-town cat Appreciate what you have	Numbers: 90, 100	Social studies: Jobs	Make a jobs poster
Units 7–9 Review Page 118–119							

Hello again!

HOSPITAL

Welcome back to *Pippa and Pop*

1 Me!

🎧³ **Listen to the song.**

1 Introduction and language review: *Hello! What's your name? I'm (Kim / Dan / Pippa / Pop / Tinks). How old are you? I'm (eight / five / six / three). I like (books / trains).*

🎧 Listen. 👆 Point. ⭕ Circle.

6 ⑧

5 4

6 7

3 5

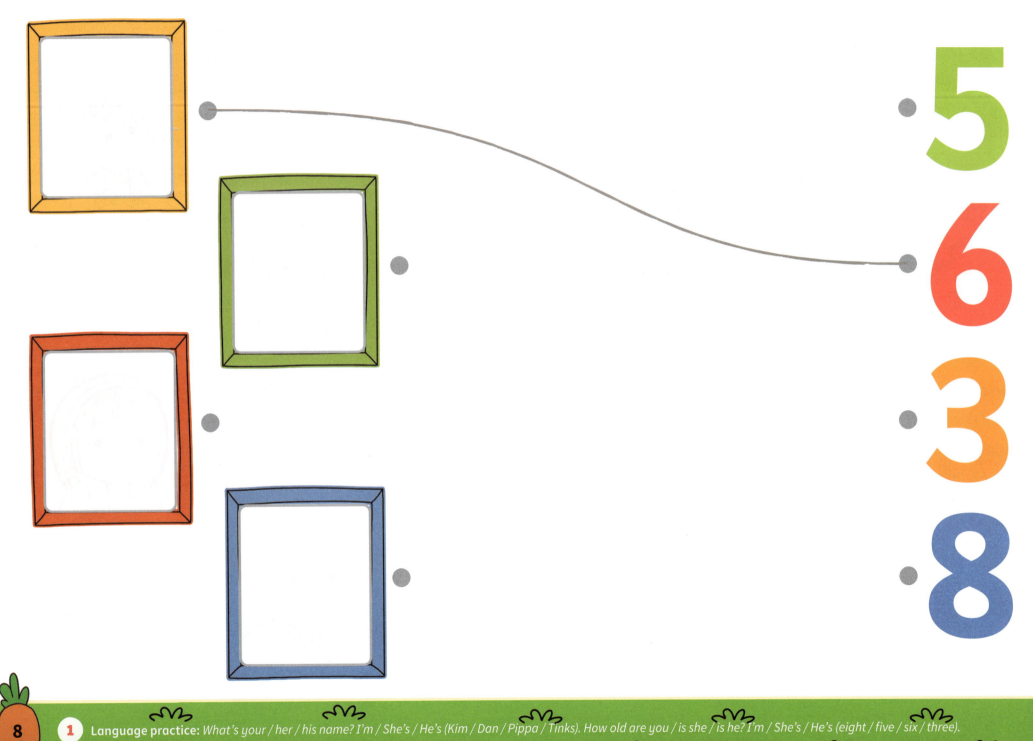

🎧 Listen. ⬭ Stick. ▮ Match. 💬 Say.

5

6

3

8

1 Language practice: *What's your / her / his name? I'm / She's / He's (Kim / Dan / Pippa / Tinks). How old are you / is she / is he? I'm / She's / He's (eight / five / six / three).*

🎧 **6 Listen.** ⭕ **Trace.** 📕 **Match.** 🗨 **Say.**

🎧 **7** **Listen.** **Jane's name**

1

2

3

4

1 Literacy

1 **Language presentation:** *He's / She's / I'm (bored / sleepy / surprised / angry / excited / scared). She isn't / He isn't / I'm not (bored).*

🎧 **Listen.** 👁 **Look.** ⭕ **Circle.** 🎵 **Sing.**

👁 **Look.** ✋ **Count.** 📕 **Match.**

1 2 3 4	10	(green dots)
6 7 8 9	20	(red dots)
11 12 13 14	5	(purple dots)
16 17 18 19	15	(yellow dots)

🎧 ¹⁰ Listen. ◯ Circle.

1

2

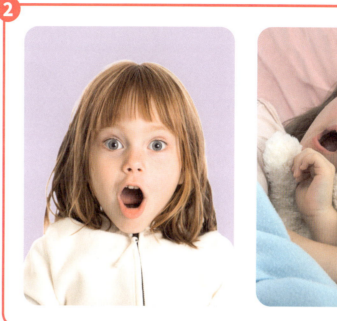

3

4

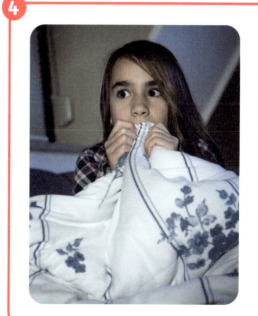 

🎧 ¹¹ **Listen.** ✏️ **Draw.** 💬 **Say.**

1

2

3

4

5

6

1 *He's / She's / I'm (bored / sleepy / surprised / angry / excited / scared). She isn't / He isn't / I'm not (bored).*

👁 **Look.** ✋ **Make.** 💬 **Say.**

What's (your) name? (I'm) (Ana). How old are you / is she / is he? I'm / She's / He's (five / six).   ①

② My day

🎧 **12 Listen to the song.**

② **Unit topic introduction:** Daily activities

🎧 Listen. 👆 Point. ⭕ Trace.

🎧 Listen. ➡️➡️ Follow. ◗ Stick. 💬 Say.

2 Language practice: *I (wake up / wash my face / get dressed / brush my hair / have breakfast / brush my teeth) every day.*

15 Listen. ◌ Trace. ○ Circle. Say.

sh

1

2

3

4

🎧17 Listen. 👆 Point. ⭕ Circle.

1

2

3

4

5

6

2 Language presentation: *They / We (play with friends / have a snack / have dinner / have a bath / listen to a story / go to bed) (after school / in the evening). We don't (have a bath).*

🎧 Listen. ✔️❌ Tick or cross. 🎵 Sing.

✋ **Count.** ✏️ **Draw.** ⭕ **Trace.** 🔴 **Say.**

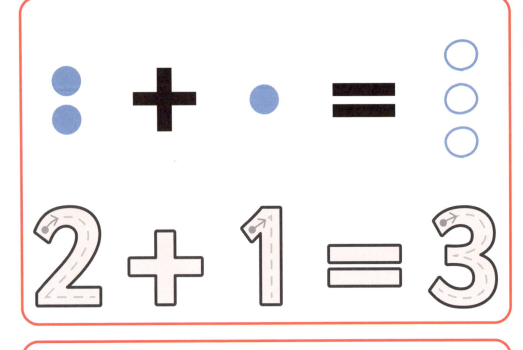

$$2 + 1 = 3$$

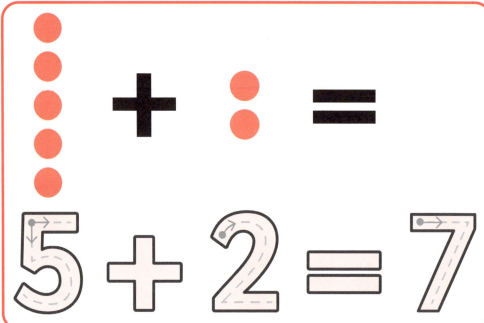

$$5 + 2 = 7$$

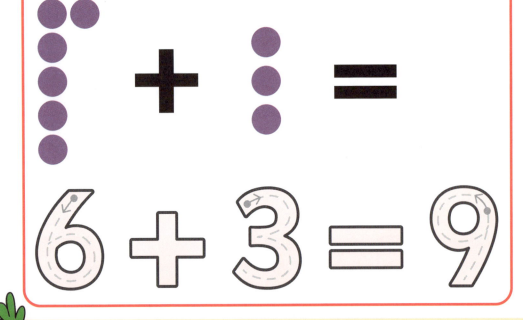

$$6 + 3 = 9$$

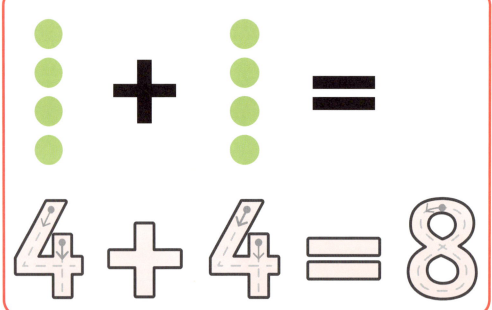

$$4 + 4 = 8$$

👁 Look. 📙 Match.

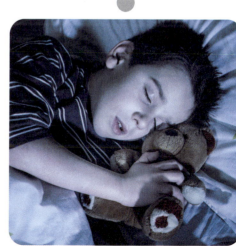

🎧 ¹⁹ Listen. 📕 Match. 💬 Say.

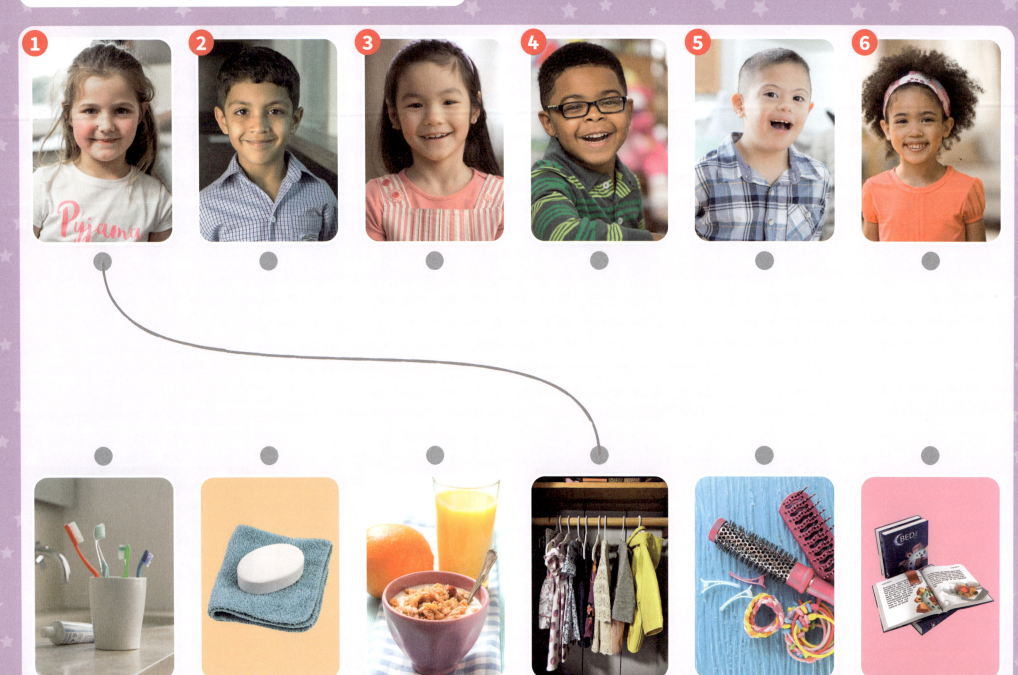

2 *I (wash my face / get dressed / brush my hair / have breakfast / brush my teeth / listen to a story) (in the morning / every day / in the evening).*

Look. Make. Say.

③ My home

🎧²⁰ **Listen to the song.**

③ Unit topic introduction: Activities in the home

🎧 ²¹ Listen. 👆 Point. ⭕ Circle.

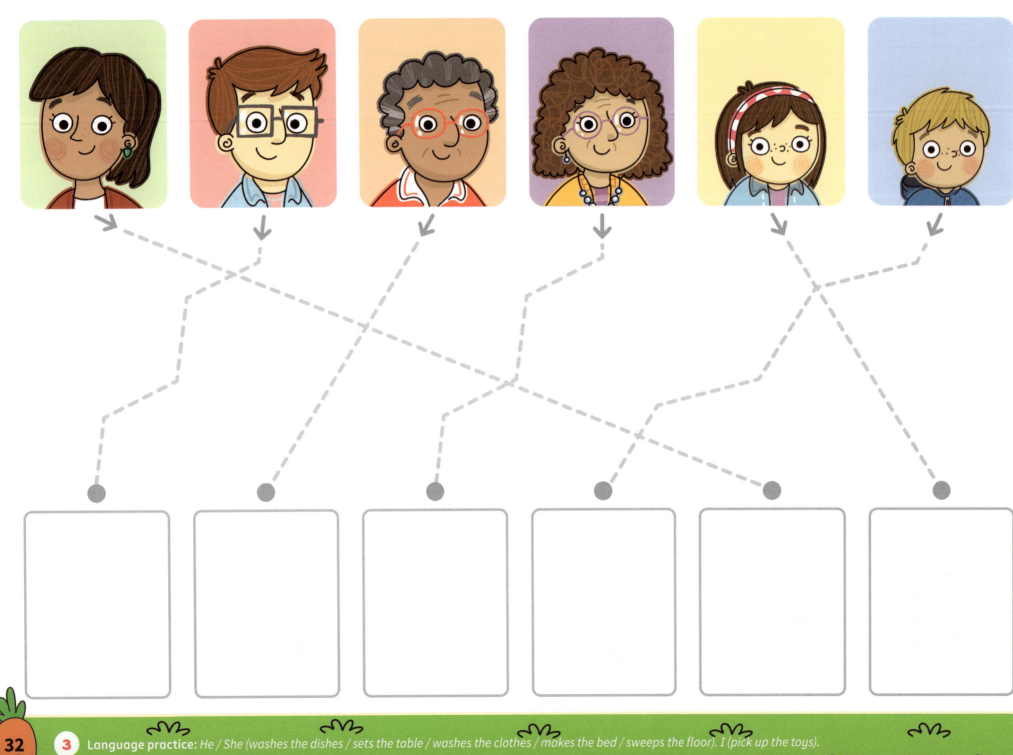

3 Language practice: *He / She (washes the dishes / sets the table / washes the clothes / makes the bed / sweeps the floor). I (pick up the toys).*

23 **Listen.** ◌ **Trace.** ○ **Circle.** ◼ **Say.**

🎧²⁴ Listen. Goldilocks and the three bears

1

2

3

4

5

6

7

8

🎧 **25** **Listen.** 👆 **Point.** 🖍 **Colour.**

3 Language presentation: *It's (under / on / in / next to) the (bed / rug / cupboard / toy box / lamp / bookcase).*

🎧 ²⁶ Listen. ✔✘ Tick or cross. 🎵 Sing.

🎧 **²⁷ Listen.** ⭕ **Trace.** ✋ **Count.** ✏️ **Colour.**

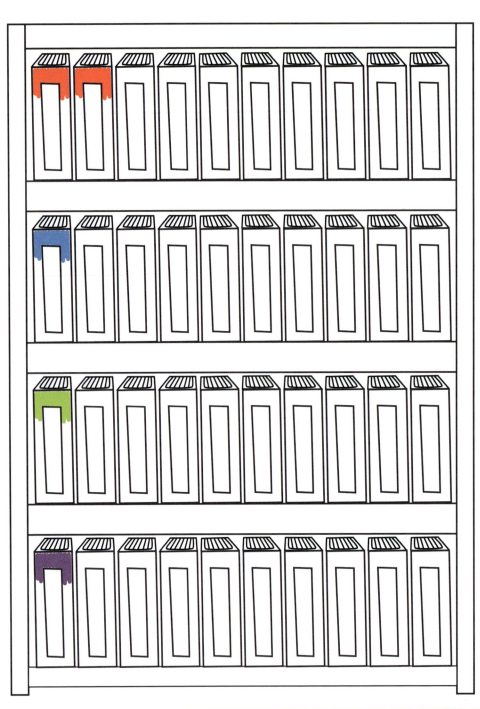

👁 Look. 🟧 Match.

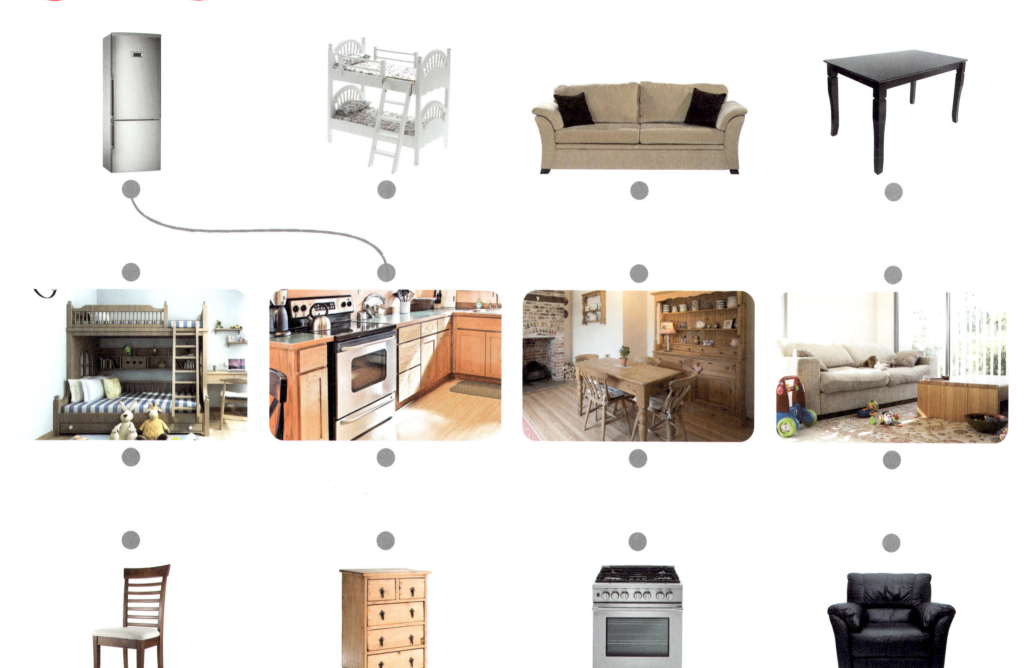

🎧28 Listen. 📙 Match. 🟥 Say.

3 *He / She (washes the dishes / picks up the toys / sets the table / washes the clothes / makes the beds / sweeps the floor) (in the morning).*

 Look. Make. Say.

🎧 29 **Listen.** 🔍 **Find.** 123 **Number.** 💬 **Say.**

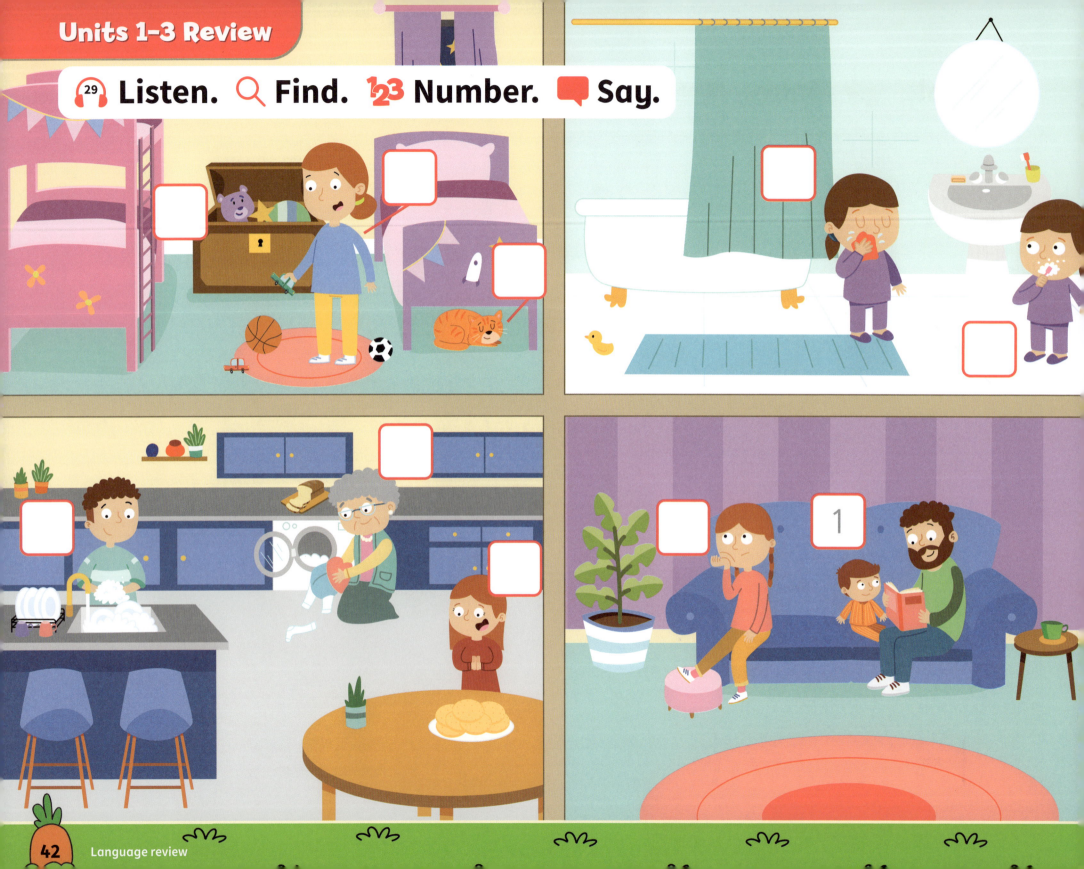

4 + 2 = 6

5 + 3 = _____

10 + 1 = _____

10 + 10 = _____

4 My sports

🎧 30 **Listen to the song.**

 4 Unit topic introduction: Sports

🎧 Listen. 👆 Point. 🔢 Number.

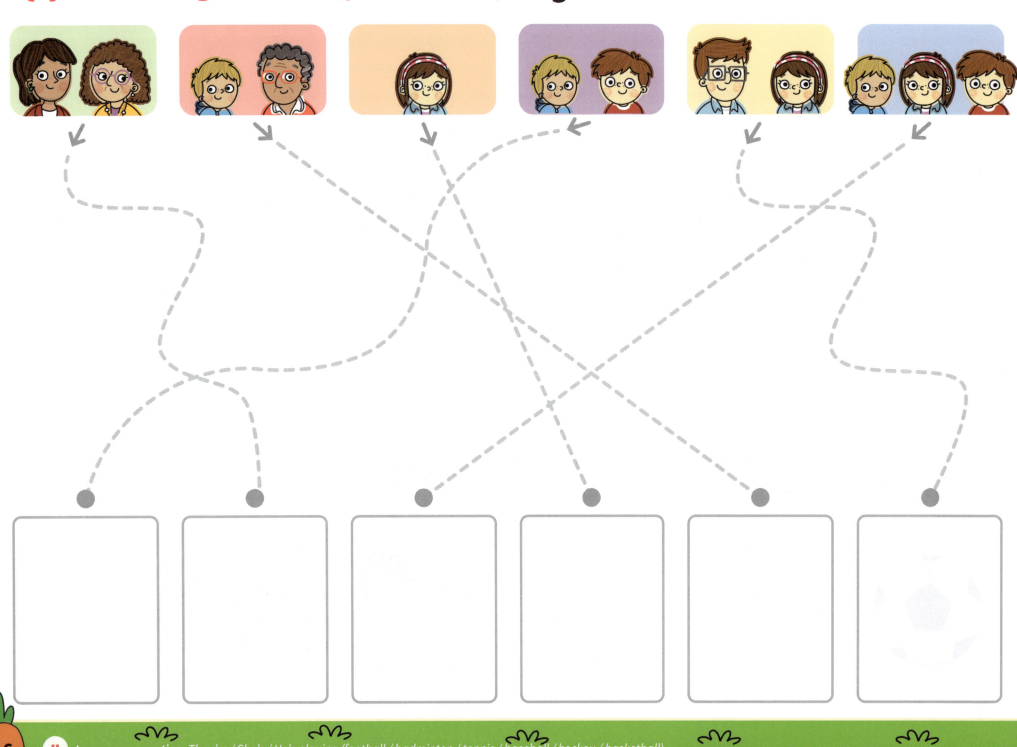

4 Language practice: *They're / She's / He's playing (football / badminton / tennis / baseball / hockey / basketball).*

🎧 ³³ **Listen.** ◌ **Trace.** ◯ **Circle.** ▣ **Say.**

ng

Listen. **A sport for Grace**

1

2

3

4

4 Language presentation: *She's / He's / They're / I'm (throwing / hitting / catching / bouncing / rolling / kicking) the ball.*

🎧 **Listen.** 👁 **Look.** ⭕ **Circle.** 🎵 **Sing.**

👋 **Count.** ✏️ **Draw.** ⭕ **Trace.** 🟥 **Say.**

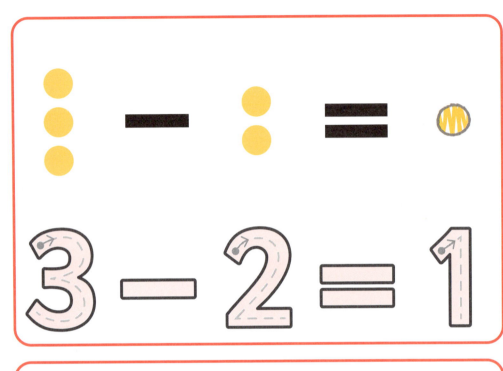

$3 - 2 = 1$

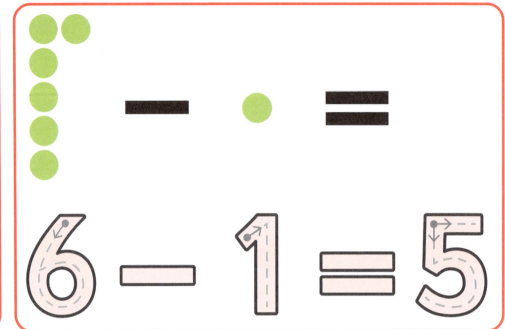

$6 - 1 = 5$

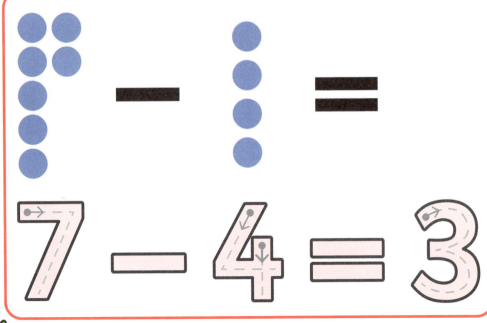

$7 - 4 = 3$

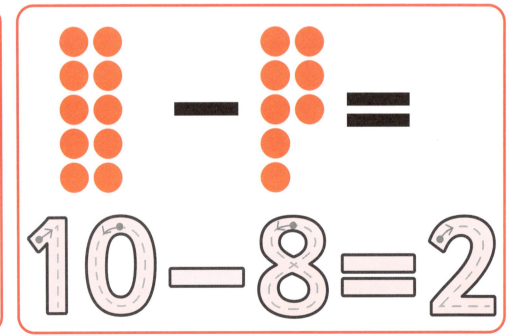

$10 - 8 = 2$

🎧 **37 Listen.** 🟥 **Match.**

9　　　11　　　5

🎧 **38 Listen.** ✔✘ **Tick or cross.** 💬 **Say.**

1

✔

2

3

4

5

6

7

8

4 *They're / She's / He's playing (football / badminton / tennis / baseball / hockey / basketball). They're / She's / He's (throwing / hitting / catching / bouncing / rolling / kicking) the ball.*

👁 **Look.** 🖐 **Make.** 😊 **Play.**

5 My free time

🎧 39 **Listen to the song.**

5 **Unit topic introduction:** Free-time activities

🎧⁴⁰ Listen. 👆 Point. 1²³ Number.

🎧 Listen. ⭕ Trace. 🏷️ Stick. 💬 Say.

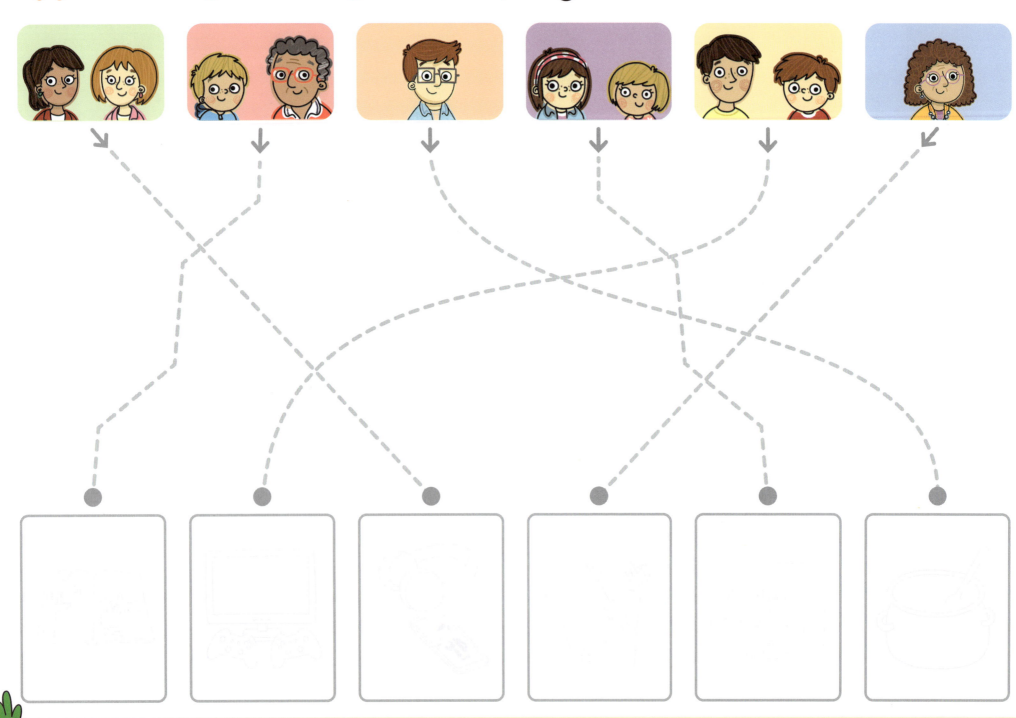

5 Language practice: *I / We like (reading books / cooking dinner / watching TV / playing video games / listening to singing / drawing pictures).*

42 🎧 **Listen.** ⬭ **Trace.** ⬭ **Circle.** ▬ **Say.**

🎧 **Listen.** Jack loves reading

1

Jack likes reading books.

2

Jack likes police officers.

3

Come and help, please.

4

Come and help, please.

Jack!

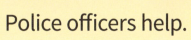

Police officers help.

I can help.

1

2

3

4

5

6

5 Language presentation: *Let's (go swimming / go roller skating / play a board game / play with building blocks / play outside / play hide-and-seek)! Can I (come / play)?*

🎧 ⁴⁵ Listen. ✔️❌ Tick or cross. 🎵 Sing.

🎧 46 **Listen.** ⭕ **Trace.** ✋ **Count.** 🟥 **Match.**

10 20 30 40 50 60

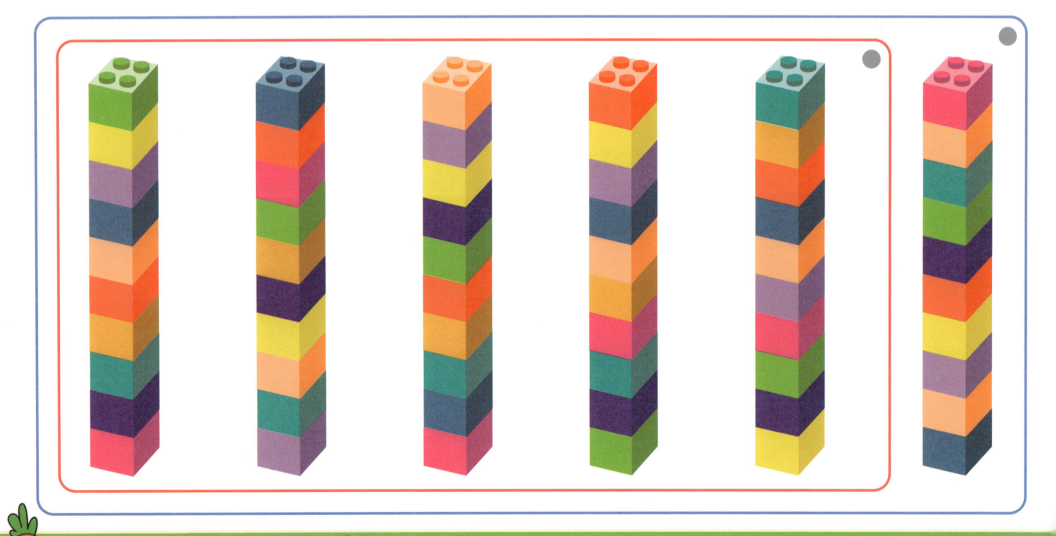

👁 Look. 📱 Match.

🎧 47 Listen. 123 Number. 💬 Say.

1

5 *I / We like (reading books / cooking dinner / watching TV / playing video games / listening to singing / drawing pictures).*

Look. Make. Play.

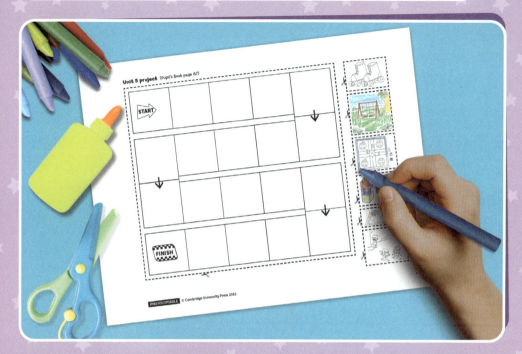

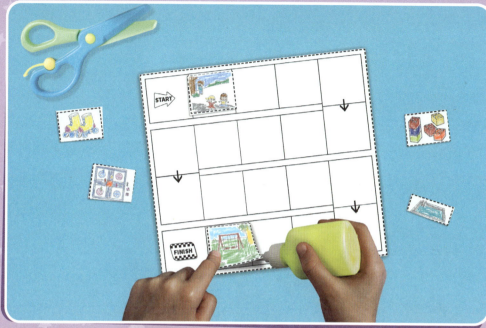

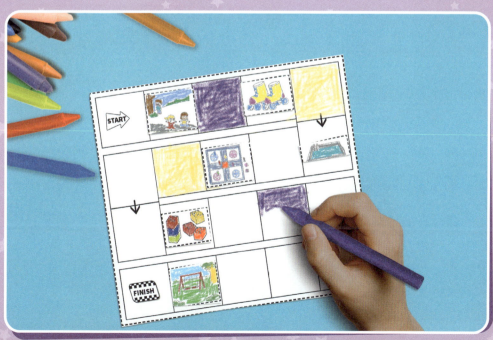

6 My food

🎧 48 **Listen to the song.**

🎧 Listen. 👆 Point. ✔✖ Tick or cross.

 Listen. Stick. Circle. Say.

1

Yes — No

2

Yes — No

3

Yes — No

4

Yes — No

5

Yes — No

6

Yes — No

6 **Language practice:** *Would you like some (chocolate / grapes / crisps / sweets / pineapple / cake)? Yes, please. / No, thank you.*

51 **Listen.** ⭕ **Trace.** ✏️ **Colour.** 🗨️ **Say.**

LISTEN. Share, Ricky Raccoon!

1 Ricky is eating the sweets.

2 Ricky is eating the ice cream.

3 Where's our ice cream?

4 Ricky is eating the cake.

5

Where's our cake?

6

Ricky is sad.

7

Let's make some biscuits.

8

Ricky is sharing!

6 Language presentation: I / We have (meat / rice / fruit / cereal / vegetables / beans / carrots) for (breakfast / lunch / dinner).

🎧 Listen. ✔✖ Tick or cross. 🎵 Sing.

🟥 **Say.** ⭕ **Circle.** ✋ **Count.** ✏️ **Write.**

10

20

30

10

20

40

60

20

30

40

10

30

50

⊙ Look. ◯ Circle.

salty

sour

sweet

 **Listen.** **Match.** **Say.**

1

2

6 *Would you like some (chocolate / grapes / crisps / sweets / pineapple / cake)? Yes, please. / No, thank you. I'd like (lots of) grapes.*

👁 Look. 🖐 Make. 💬 Say.

56 🎧 Listen. 🔍 Find. 123 Number. 💬 Say.

✋ **Count.** ✏️ **Draw.** ✏️ **Write.**

6 − 3 = 3

8 − 2 = ___

10 − 7 = ___

9 − 5 = ___

7 Animals

Listen to the song.

7 Unit topic introduction: Wild animals

🎧 58 Listen. 👆 Point. 1̣2̣3̣ Number.

tigers

crocodile

elephants

1

1

2

3

4

7

hippos

monkeys

snake

7 Language practice: *There's (a crocodile / a snake). There are (two) (tigers / monkeys / hippos / elephants). There are lots of (monkeys).*

60 Listen. ◯ Trace. ◯ Circle. 🟥 Say.

13

3

10

🎧 [61] Listen. The bird and the lion

1

The bird sees a big lion.

2

3

4

The lion wakes up!

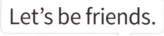

Giraffes!

7 **Language presentation:** *They're (giraffes / zebras / ducks / parrots / lizards / spiders). They've got (long necks / long legs / stripes / short legs / big feet / long tails). They're (fast).*

🎧 63 **Listen.** ⭕ **Trace.** ✏️ **Colour.** 🎵 **Sing.**

Listen. Trace. Count. Colour.

10 20 30 40 50 60 70 80

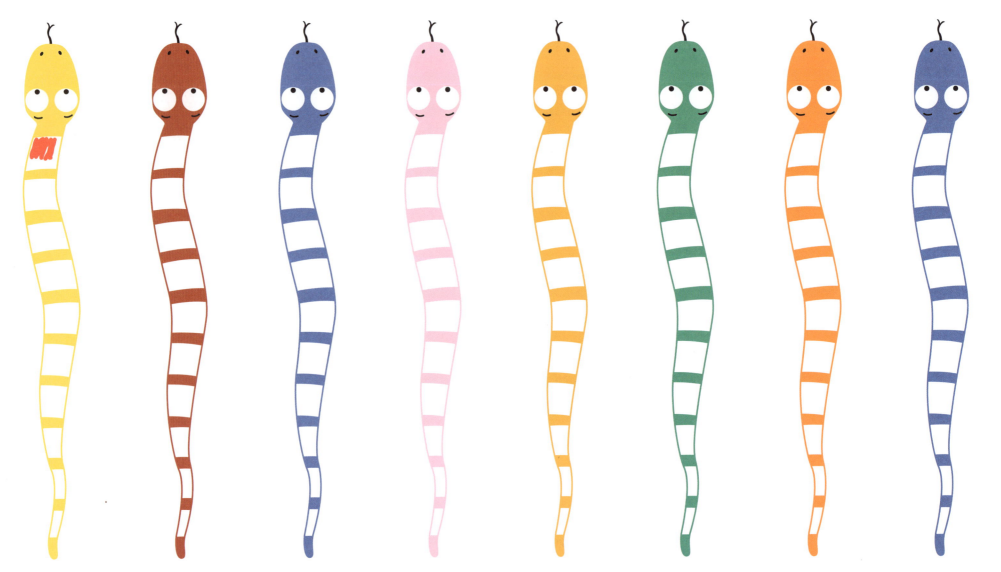

7 Numbers: *70, 80*

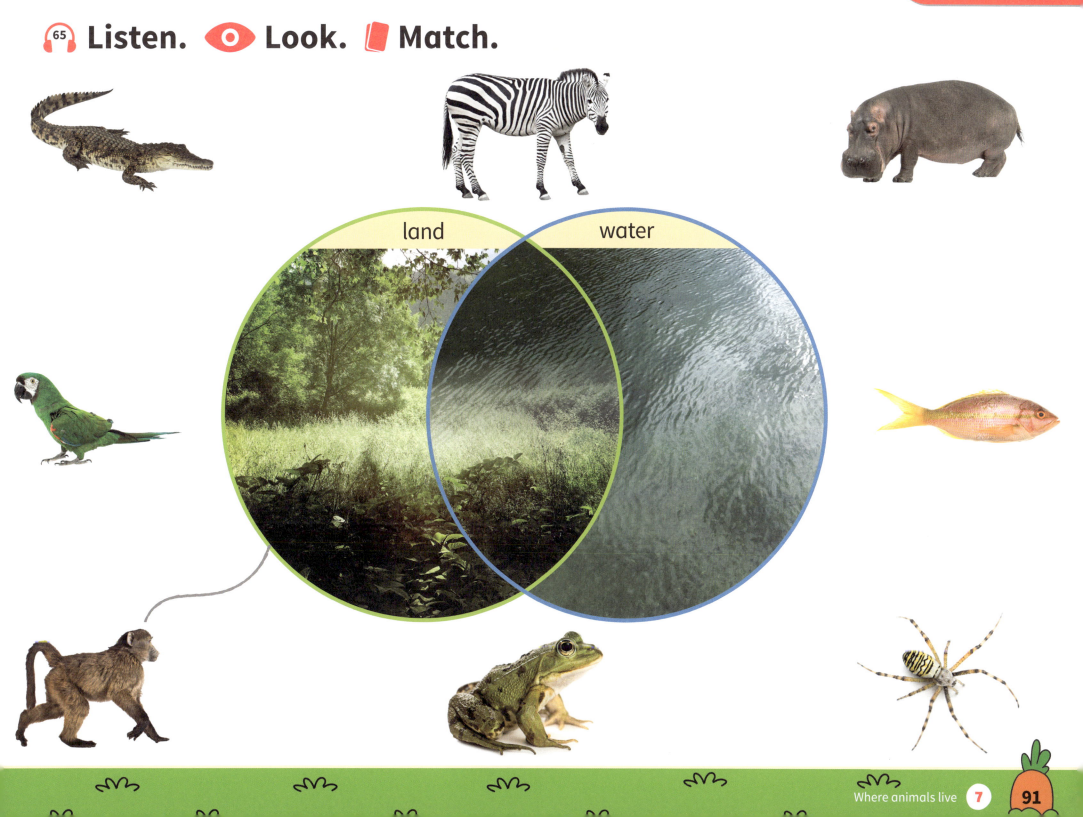

🎧 65 **Listen.** 👁 **Look.** 📙 **Match.**

land   water

🎧 66 Listen. ⭕ Circle. 💬 Say.

1

parrots

lizards

2

zebras

hippos

3

ducks

crocodiles

4

giraffes

elephants

7 *They're (giraffes / zebras / ducks / parrots / lizards / crocodiles / hippos / elephants). They've got (long necks / long legs / stripes / short legs / long tails / sharp teeth / small ears).*

👁 **Look.** 🙌 **Make.** 💬 **Say.**

8 Plants

67 **Listen to the song.**

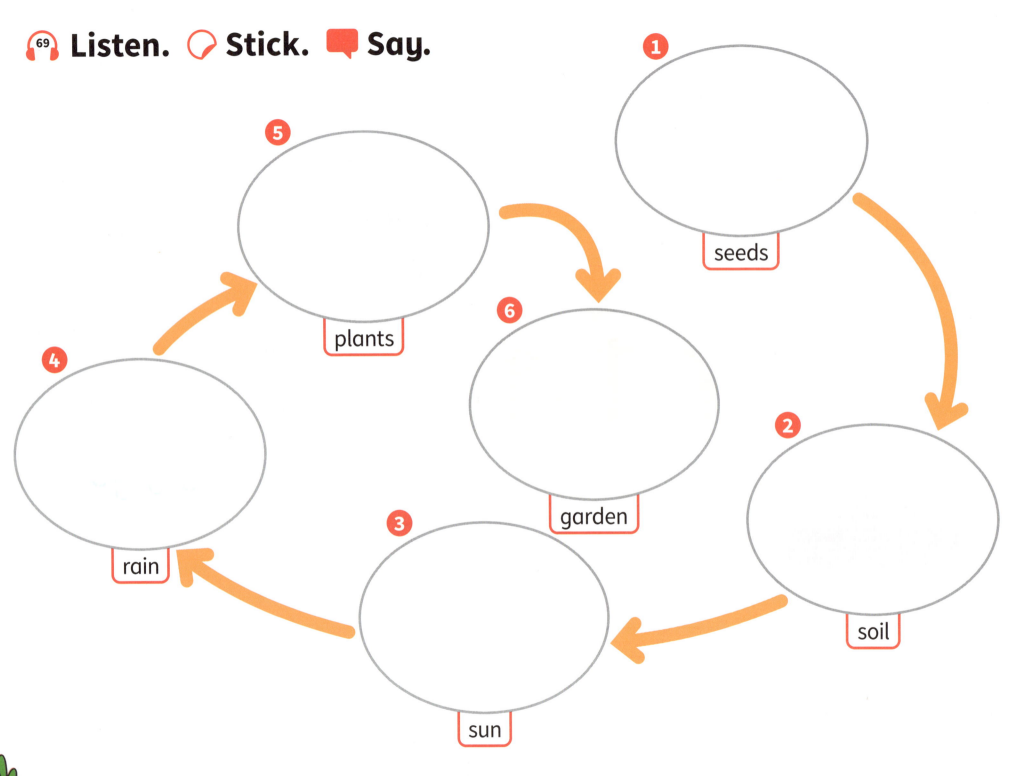

🎧 [69] Listen. ⬭ Stick. 💬 Say.

1 seeds

2 soil

3 sun

4 rain

5 plants

6 garden

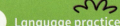

70 🎧 **Listen.** ⭕ **Trace.** ⭕ **Circle.** 🔲 **Say.**

🎧 Listen. Sophia and Sam's garden

1

Sophia and Sam want a garden.

2

Sophia and Sam are talking.

3

Sophia gives her plants water.

4

Plants need sun.

5 Sam puts his plants in the sun.

6 Plants need water.

7 The plants grow and grow.

8 What a beautiful garden!

Listen. 👆 Point. ⭕ Circle.

What a dirty nose!

8 **Language presentation:** *beautiful, dirty, ugly, new, old, clean; What (beautiful) flowers! What (a dirty) (nose)!*

🎧⁷³ Listen. ✔✖ Tick or cross. 🎵 Sing.

beautiful ✔

ugly ☐

beautiful ☐

dirty ☐

new ☐

new ☐

old ☐

dirty ☐

clean ☐

 Look. Count. Write.

2

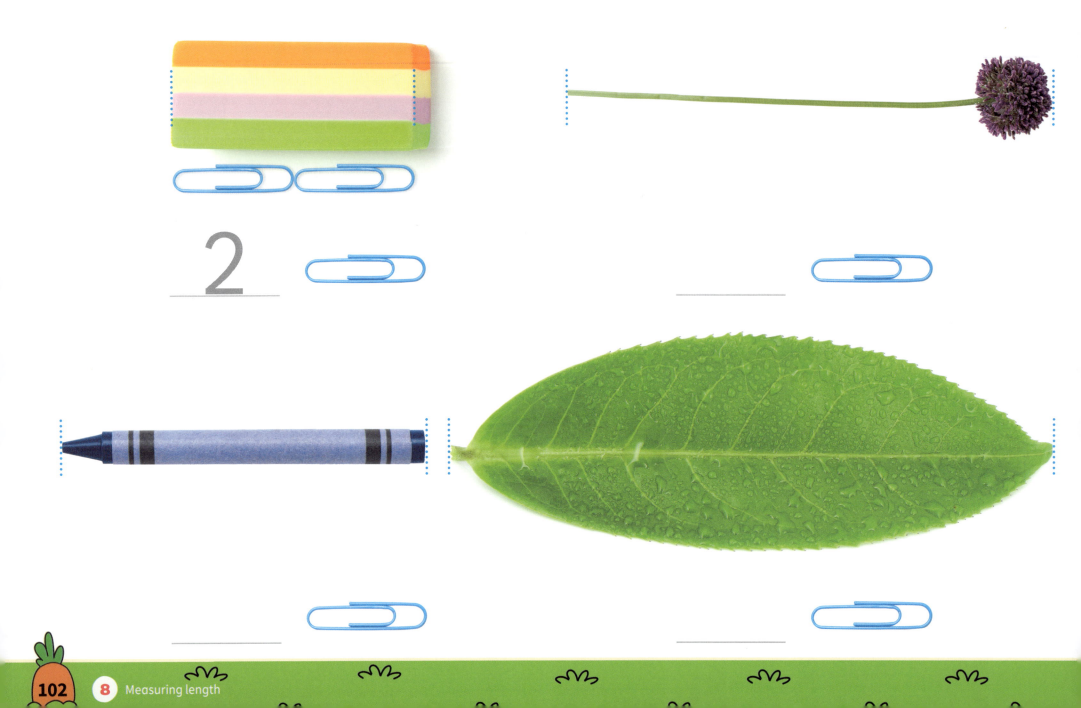

👁 Look. 1̃23 Number.

🎧 **Listen.** ⭕ **Circle.** 💬 **Say.**

1

2

3

4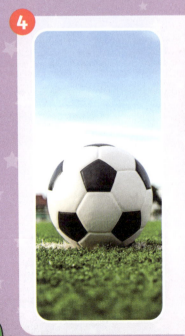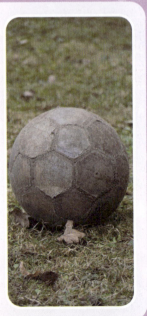

5

6

8 *beautiful, dirty, ugly, new, old, clean; What (dirty) (hands)! What (an ugly) (beach)!*

👁 **Look.** 🖐 **Make.** 💬 **Say.**

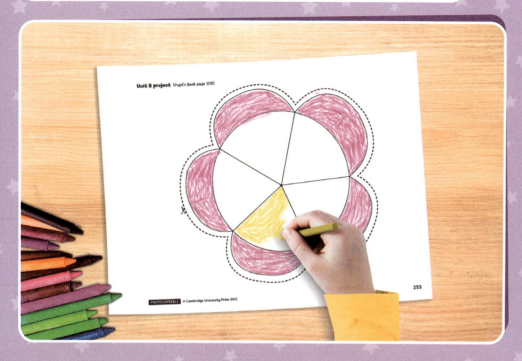

Plants need sun.

⑨ My town

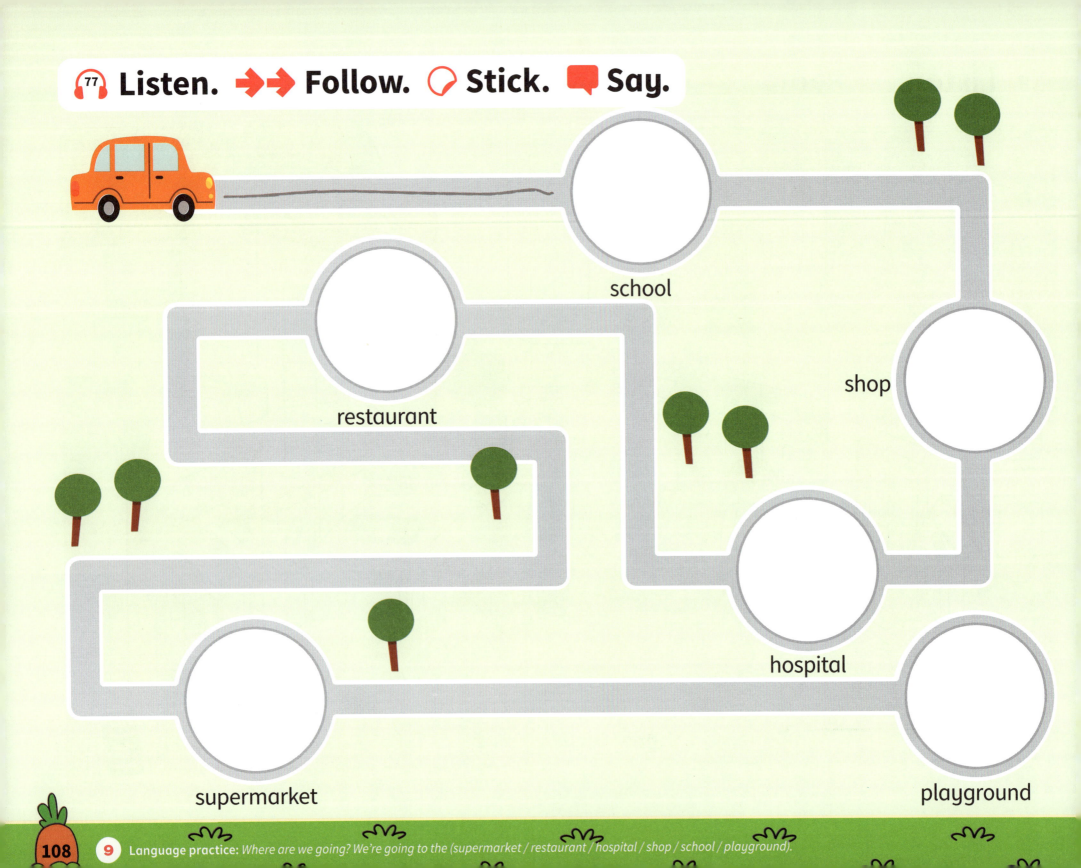

🎧 **77 Listen.** ➡️➡️ **Follow.** ⬭ **Stick.** 🔲 **Say.**

school

restaurant

shop

hospital

supermarket

playground

9 Language practice: *Where are we going? We're going to the (supermarket / restaurant / hospital / shop / school / playground).*

78 🎧 Listen. 🔴 Trace. 🔵 Circle. 💬 Say.

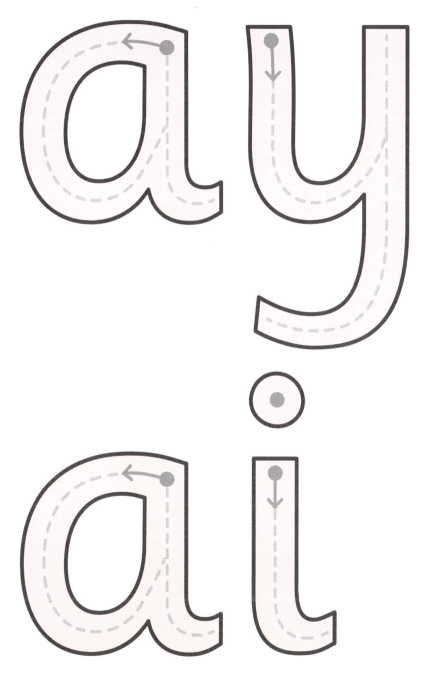

It's very loud.

Run!

I'm scared.

I don't like the big city.

Ben and Bill say goodbye.

Listen. Point. Circle.

1

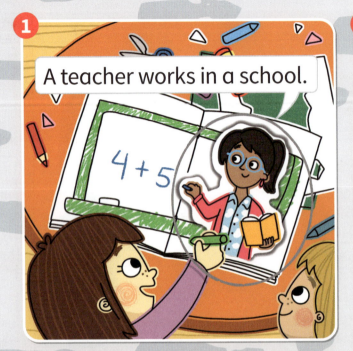

A teacher works in a school.

2

3

4

5

6

9 Language presentation: *teacher, doctor, nurse, farmer, waiter, shop assistant; (A teacher) works (in) a (school). Does (a nurse) work (in) a (hospital)? Yes, (she) does. No, (she) doesn't.*

🎧⁸¹ Listen. 📕 Match. 🎵 Sing.

teacher　　farmer　　doctor　　waiter　　shop assistant　　nurse

🎧 **Listen.** ⭕ **Trace.** ✋ **Count.** 🖊 **Colour.**

20 **40** **60** **80** **100**

10 **30** **50** **70** **90**

🎧 ⁸³ Listen. 👁 Look. ✔✘ Tick or cross.

1

✔

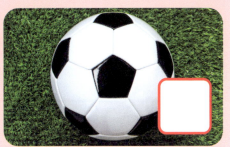

2

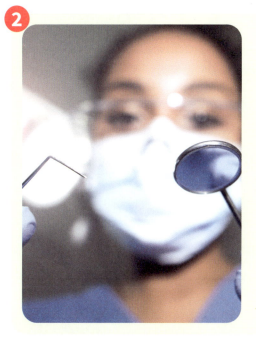

3

4

🎧 84 Listen. 🔍 Find. 1̲2̲3 Number. 💬 Say.

9 *Where are we going? We're going to the (supermarket / restaurant / hospital / shop / school / playground).*

Look. Make. Say.

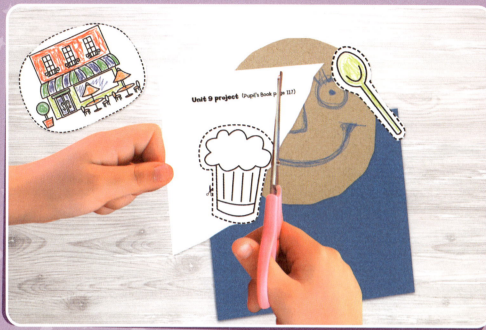

Unit 9 project *(Pupil's Book page 117)*

A cook works in a restaurant.

🎧 **Listen.** 🔍 **Find.** 🔢 **Number.** 💬 **Say.**

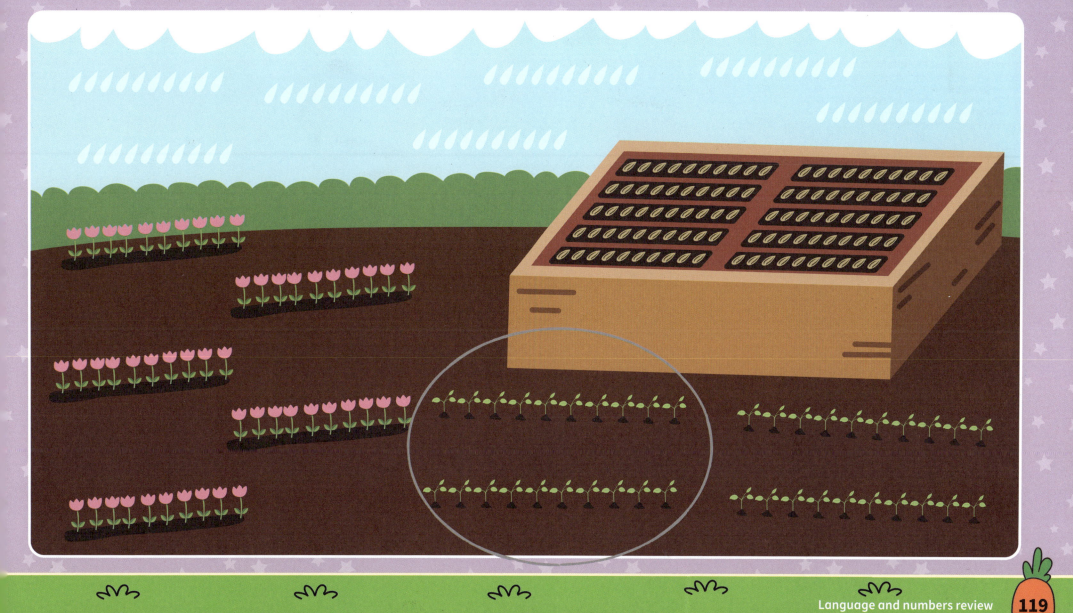

Look. Count. Circle.

20 🌱 40 🌷 60 100 🌰

Thanks and Acknowledgements

Authors' thanks
Many thanks to everyone at Cambridge University Press for their dedication and hard work in extraordinarily complicated circumstances, and in particular to:
Liane Grainger for her unwavering professionalism and her irrepressible joviality;
Emily Hird for her endless enthusiasm, good humour and sound judgement;
Jane Holt for her unflagging energy and her ability to bring the whole, sprawling project together;
Vanessa Gold for her hard work and sound editorial contribution.
Catherine Ball, Stephanie Howard and Carolyn Wright for their hard work helping to review, correct and knead the manuscript into shape.

Our thoughts and hearts go out to all the teachers and their pupils who have suffered and continue to suffer the devastating effects of the global pandemic that has changed all our lives. Stay strong.

Dedications
For my darling 'ladies', Lydia and Silvia, with much love – CN
For Paloma, Pablo and Carlota, keep on smiling, love - MT
Caroline Nixon and Michael Tomlinson, Murcia, Spain

The publishers and authors would like to thank the following contributors:
Additional writing by Lesley Koustaff, Susan Rivers and Catherine Ball.
Book design and page make-up by Blooberry Design.
Cover design and illustrations by Blooberry Design; QBS Learning.
Cover photography by NYS444/iStock/Getty Images Plus.
Commissioned photography by Blooberry Design.
Freelance editing by Catherine Ball, Stephanie Howard and Carolyn Wright.
Audio recording and production by Leon Chambers.
Original songs and chants composition by Robert Lee.
Songs and chants production by Jake Carter.
Animation production by QBS Learning and Collaborate Agency.

The authors and publishers acknowledge the following sources of copyright material and are grateful for the permissions granted. While every effort has been made, it has not always been possible to identify the sources of all the material used or to trace all copyright holders.
 If any omissions are brought to our notice, we will be happy to include the appropriate acknowledgments on reprinting and in the next update to the digital edition, as applicable.

Key: U = Unit.

Photographs

All photos are sourced from Getty Images.
U1: Mike Kemp; Westend61; FatCamera/E+; Asya_mix/iStock/Getty Images Plus; Lubushka/iStock/Getty Images Plus; Manop Boonpeng/EyeEm; Antagain/E+; Richard Newstead/Moment; FRANCOIS-EDMOND/iStock/Getty Images Plus; GlobalP/iStock/Getty Images Plus; ElementalImaging/iStock/Getty Images Plus; PhotoAlto/Laurence Mouton; Stockbyte; Roland Magnusson/EyeEm; Nirut Punshiri/EyeEm; Irina_Strelnikova/iStock/Getty Images Plus; Jose luis Pelaez Inc/Digital Vision; Imgorthand/E+; Juanmonino/istock; Lea Paterson/Science Photo Library; Caroline schiff/Terta Images; Westend 61; Ideabug/istock; Mai Vu/iStock/Getty Images Plus; **U2:** skynesher/E+; Kelvin Murray/Photodisc; 5m3photos/Moment; Corbis/VCG; Tetra Images; barleyman/Moment; Brian Mitchell/Corbis Documentary; Sally Anascombe/Stone; PhotoNotebook/iStock/Getty Images Plus; iStock/Getty Images Plus; Chris Hackett/Tetra Images; Jose A. Bernat Bacete/Moment; Jiri V'aclavek/EyeEm; Kyoshino/istock; Moyo Studio/E+; Peopleimages/E+; Jose Luis Pelaez Inc/Digital Vision; Deyangeorgiev/istock; Solstock/istock; Zubbin Shroof/The Image bank; Ariel Skelley/Digital Vision; SDI Productions/E+; Image Source; eurobanks/iStock/Getty Images Plus; Elinamaninen/istock; Secret agent mike/moment; Serezniy/istock; Pictofoloia/E+; **U3:** Imagenavi; Ake1150sb/istock; Uwe krejci/istock; Explora_2005/istock; Juzant/digital vision; John Keeble/Moment; Mint Images RF; Grenme/istock; Ednam/istock; JazzIRT/E+; Creatikon Studio/istock; Atiati/E+; YangYin/E+; Skrow/E+; Luminis/istock; Luis Alvarez/DigitalVision; Westend 61; Bonnie Tarpey - Wronski/EyeEm; Bobbieo/istock; Gabe Palmer/The Image Bank; Emyerson/istock; Kevin trimmer/Moment; Dazeley/The Image Bank; Brizmaker/Getty Images; Martin Poole/The Image bank; Carolyn Hebbard/Moment Open; Shestock; **U4:** Lorado/E+; Imgorthand/E+; Peter cade/Stone; Thomas Barwick/Digital Vision; FatCamera/E+; Ariel Skelley/DigitalVision; Amstockphoto/istock; Jill Former/Photographer RF choice; Pongnathee Kluaythong/EyeEm; C Squared Studios/Photodisc; Barcin/istock; Kinzie Riehm/Image Source; Peter Titmuss/Universal Images Group; Dennis Lane; Sam Edwards/OJO Images; JLBarranco/E+; Pekic/E+; David Madison/Stone; Tim Clayton - Corbis; **U5:** ViewStock; BraunS/E+; Johner Images; MsMoloko/iStock/Getty Images Plus; Fuse/Corbis; Gary John Norman/Cultura; Mark Douet/The Image Bank/Getty Images Plus; Eric Lafforgue/Art in All of Us/Corbis; thenakedsnail/Moment/Getty Images Plus; Steve Jennings/WireImage; Richard T. Nowitz/The Image Bank; oxygen/Russia; Tomekbudujedomek/Moment; Hiroshi Higuchi/The Image Bank; Jim Spoontz/Stringer/Getty Images Sport; Tim Hall/Cultura; LittleBee80/iStock/Getty Images Plus; Westend61; Prostock-Studio/iStock/Getty Images Plus; AleksandarNakic/E+; **U6:** Morsa Images/DigitalVision; NWphotoguy/E+; Image Source; Peter Dazeley/Photodisc; artisteer/iStock/Getty Images Plus; Brian Macdonald/DigitalVision; Foodcollection; HandmadePictures/iStock/Getty Images Plus; belchonock/iStock/Getty Images Plus; Foodcollection RF; bombuscreative/iStock/Getty Images Plus; margouillatphotos/; Rani Sr Prasiththi/EyeEm; Sutin Yuukung/EyeEm; Alexandra Grablewski/Photodisc; The Picture Pantry/Alloy; MIXA; FGorgun/iStock/Getty Images Plus; gangnavigator/iStock/Getty Images Plus; Petra Matjasic/EyeEm; Sarah-Jane Blackah/EyeEm; Zen Rial/Moment; Bloxsome Photography/Moment; byryo/iStock/Getty Images Plus; **U7:** Peter Unger/Stone; Vicki Jauron, Babylon and Beyond Photography/Moment; Mike Hill/Stone; Tatsiana Volskaya/Moment; Vera Buerkle/EyeEm; avi11/E+; Theo Allofs/Stockbyte; Nneka Mckay/EyeEm; Peter Groenendijk/robertharding; Aditya Singh; kuritafsheen/RooM; Lutfi Hanafi/EyeEm; Mikel Cornejo/EyeEm; Xuanyu Han/Moment; vusta/E+; DaddyBit/iStock/Getty Images Plus; GlobalP/iStock/Getty Images Plus; Brian Hagiwara/The Image Bank; Martin Harvey/The Image Bank; George Doyle & Ciaran Griffin/Stockbyte; Yuxin Xiao/500px; By Eve Livesey/Moment; SG Wildlife Photography/500px/500Px Plus; StuPorts/iStock/Getty Images Plus; Nick Dale/EyeEm; Manoj Shah/Photodisc; Manoj Shah/Stone; Simon Phelps Photography/Moment; **U8:** Neumann & Rodtmann/The Image Bank; sarayut Thaneerat/Moment; Eskay Lim/EyeEm; temmuzcan/iStock/Getty Images Plus; Paula French/EyeEm; mikroman6/Moment; temmuzcan/E+; Studio Light and Shade/iStock/Getty Images Plus; taketan/Moment; Westend61; Liliboas/E+; Richard Sharrocks/Moment; AtlasStudio/iStock/Getty Images Plus; ihorga/iStock/Getty Images Plus; EHStock/iStock/Getty Images Plus; akepong/iStock/Getty Images Plus; Richard Clark/The Image Bank; Libby Hipkins/Moment; Yanuar Sudrajat/EyeEm; ClarkandCompany/iStock/Getty Images Plus; Tetsuya Tanooka/Aflo; Rachel Weill/UpperCut Images; Stefan Cristian Cioata/Moment; Kate Kunz/Corbis; Freer Law/iStock/Getty Images Plus; Matteo Colombo/Moment; tunart/E+; Ohmega1982/iStock/Getty Images Plus; Rolfo Brenner/EyeEm; Nicolae Gherasim/EyeEm; docksnflipflops/iStock/Getty Images Plus; Kameleon007/iStock/Getty Images Plus; FotografiaBasica/E+; **U9:** Betsie Van Der Meer/Stone; Reza Estakhrian/The Image Bank; aldomurillo/E+; Hispanolistic/E+; stoonn/iStock/Getty Images Plus; SCI_InDy/iStock/Getty Images Plus; Dina Alfasi/EyeEm; levente bodo/Moment; Massimo Borchi/Atlantide Phototravel/Corbis Documentary; Andrew Peacock/Stone; Jose Luis Pelaez Inc/DigitalVision; Fridholm, Jakob; londoneye/iStock/Getty Images Plus; C Squared Studios/Photodisc; YinYang/E+; 4x6/E+; mediaphotos/E+; stockvisual/iStock/Getty Images Plus; amstockphoto/iStock/Getty Images Plus; Peter Cade/Stone; AnthonyRosenberg/iStock/Getty Images Plus; Fuse/Corbis; Ariel Skelley/DigitalVision; Vlad Fishman/Moment; YinYang/iStock/Getty Images Plus; Kali9/E+; Maskot; Aaron Foster/DigitalVision.

Illustrations
Amy Zhing; Beatriz Castro; Begoña Corbalán; Blooberry Design; Dean Gray; Louise Farshaw; Noopur Thakur; Collaborate Agency artists; QBS Learning artists.

1 Me! (Page 8)

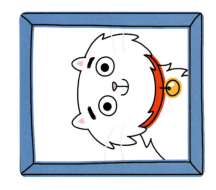

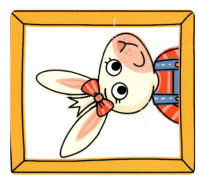

2 My day (Page 20)

3 My home (Page 32)

4 My sports (Page 46)

5 My free time (Page 58)

6 My food (Page 70)

6 My food (Page 70)

7 Animals (Page 84)

 **8 Plants** (Page 96)

 **9 My town** (Page 108)